ABANDONED
BALTIMORE

WITHDRAWN

ABANDONED BALTIMORE
SOUTHSIDE

CHRISTOPHER HALL

For the city of Baltimore, the greatest city in America

America Through Time is an imprint of Fonthill Media LLC
www.through-time.com
office@through-time.com

Published by Arcadia Publishing by arrangement with Fonthill Media LLC
For all general information, please contact Arcadia Publishing:
Telephone: 843-853-2070
Fax: 843-853-0044
E-mail: sales@arcadiapublishing.com
For customer service and orders:
Toll-Free 1-888-313-2665

www.arcadiapublishing.com

First published 2019

Copyright © Christopher Hall 2019

ISBN 978-1-63499-190-2

All rights reserved. No part of this publication may be reproduced, stored in a retrieval system or transmitted in any form or by any means, electronic, mechanical, photocopying, recording or otherwise, without prior permission in writing from Fonthill Media LLC

Typeset in Trade Gothic 10pt on 15pt
Printed and bound in England

PREFACE

Photography started for me at the age of twelve when I was given a point-and-shoot to take photos on a trip overseas with the People to People Student Ambassador Program. I fell in love with the ability to capture and share different moments from my own perspective. The release of Instagram as a platform fueled my desire to take pictures. I began to learn what I could on my own, with much guidance given to me from the tech team at Hedgesville Church in Hedgesville, West Virginia, where my family resided at the time. At the age of fourteen, with the goal to purchase my own DSLR, I started my own business selling prints and offering photoshoot services. It was at the age of sixteen when I realized photography would be what I wanted to do for the rest of my life.

In 2016, when my family moved to North Beach, Maryland, I began to take interest in photographing abandoned places. Having only lived in the area for a couple of weeks, researching places to shoot led to finding an abandoned mental asylum located about an hour away. Setting out with a friend I had just met, we ventured into the abandoned campus. On the first visit, we only explored a small portion of one out of the twenty-two buildings on the property. That was all it took for me. Urban exploring (Urbex for short) became my passion. I was fascinated by the smell of asbestos and the sound of chipped lead paint crackling beneath my feet as I walked down halls of these structures that had been seemingly forgotten about.

Currently enrolled at Maryland Institute College of Art in Baltimore, I am surrounded by a city infected with abandonment. Streets are lined with boarded up rowhomes, resembling that of an apocalyptic environment. There are an estimated 16,000 vacant buildings in the city of Baltimore, with thousands more not even accounted for. While numbers can only do so much justice, seeing and experiencing these incredible structures first hand is something hard to put in words. You have to see it to believe it. In *Abandoned Baltimore: Southside*, I made it a goal to bring awareness to this epidemic at hand. For this book, I focused mainly on places that are below Route 40, which runs directly through the middle of the city; places above Route 40 are featured in my other book, *Abandoned Baltimore: Northside*.

Of course, this book would have never been possible without several individuals. Foremost I would like to thank my parents for supporting me through everything; it means a lot. I would also like to thank the Farrell family for many childhood memories, which sparked my desire for adventure. Also, Mr. Quin and Mrs. Radosevic, my two photography teachers in high school who encouraged me to follow my passion as an artist and guide me to where I am today. Furthermore, I am incredibly grateful for all the urban explorers and photographers I have met along the way. There are countless memories with many of you that I will never forget. Finally, I would like to give a shout out and thanks to some of the original Baltimore explorers who have been exploring the city way longer than I have. Thank you Athan Serdenes, Michael Mason, Brett Robinson, Zach Brazle, and Todd Dalgliesh for all of your help and support along this journey. Finally, thank you to Fonthill Media for this unique opportunity to showcase my work.

CONTENTS

    Preface **5**

1 Town Ruins **9**

2 The Hospital and Asylum **19**

3 Remains of War **40**

4 Schools **49**

5 Rowhomes and Housing **56**

6 Industrial **68**

7 Business and More **86**

    Bibliography **96**

1

TOWN RUINS

A town must have a feature that convinces people to stay, so what happens when that no longer exists to draw people in? The gold rush is a prime example of towns that were once built that almost vanished in an instant when the resource they were searching for ran out. On the outskirts of Baltimore lies two towns situated right next to each other that suffered a similar demise. Today, only bits and pieces remain of these once-bustling areas. It is a sad sight to see and makes you wonder what life would have been like there during the time of their existence.

The very small town of Ilchester was once home to St. Mary's College. Opening in the 1890s, the college prepared hundreds of men to become ministers, priests, or rabbi. In the 1950s, the college moved to a new facility, and the original building became abandoned. Over time, people came to explore this structure and it quickly began to deteriorate, becoming a victim of vandalism. Over 100 years later, in 1997, the building and much of the property was destroyed by a fire. Some exterior structures of the main building remained until it was taken down in the mid-2000s.

Today, people come far and wide to visit the Hell House Altar. Left behind from the college, it is an altar that was used to house a large cross, which became a mysterious place where Satanists were known to worship; dark energy is said to surround the area of Ilchester because of this. The cross was eventually stolen and only the exterior of the altar is left, but that does not stop people from coming to visit this ominous place. On the adjacent hill sits a few abandoned houses from people who eventually left after the college closed. These houses have also become a victim to vandals and are almost completely covered in graffiti on the inside. This is all that remains of the small town of Ilchester, which was once home to hundreds of college students and faculty.

A little further down the road from the Hell House Altar lies the abandoned town of Daniels. The town was established along the Patapsco River in 1810 by Thomas

Ely, who built a textile mill there. Houses began to spring up around the area, and Daniels became a prosperous community. Being home to about ninety families, the town was complete with a school, churches, stores, and even its own train station. The textile mill closed in the 1960s, and everyone decided to pack up their bags and leave. In 1972, tropical storm Agnes hit the region and much of the town was flooded, causing a lot of damage, which led to the small town becoming entirely abandoned.

Most of the buildings in Daniels are gone, but a few are still standing. When I visited the town, I found a few foundations, some church ruins, and some old cars. The Saint Stanislaus Kostka Church still has some of the its stone wall still standing, along with a small graveyard that has had little to no upkeep. Further into town lies an outer shell of the Pentecostal Holiness Church, which has been tagged in graffiti.

Right: The Hell House Alter on a cold, foggy morning.

Below: An abandoned house on top of a steep hill overlooking the valley below.

What is left of an old shed outside of the house.

Inside, only a chair remains in the living room.

Above: The slightly unstable stairs that led up to the second floor.

Right: What looks like to be a little girl's room at one time.

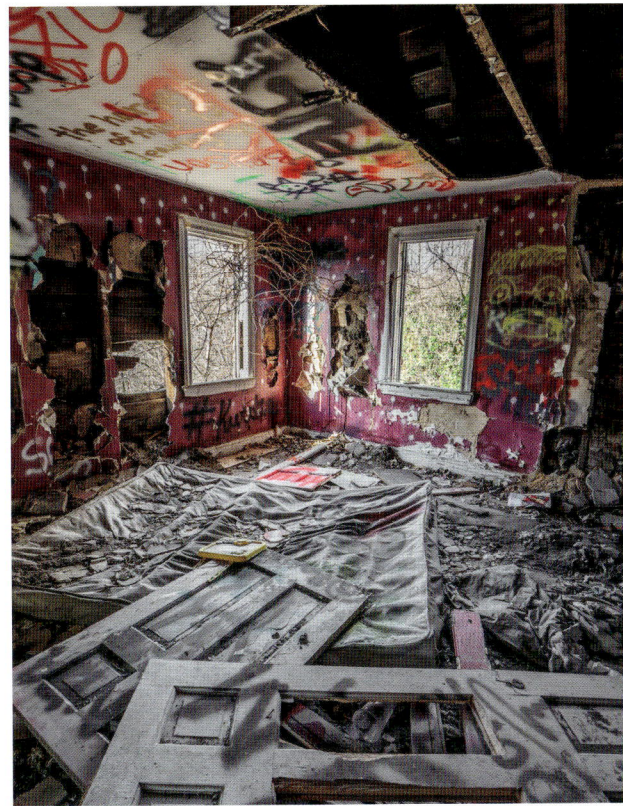

Not much remains of the few original houses that were built here.

The second abandoned home that sits further up the hill.

Some green carpet can still be seen in this also green painted room.

Every inch of the two houses were covered in graffiti.

Above: The empty shell of the Pentecostal Holiness Church.

Left: Some old tires and a car that have become part of the stream that runs down the mountain.

The front end of an old car.

The stone structure that once was the Saint Stanislaus Kostka Church.

Old grave stones from a graveyard next to the Saint Stanislaus Kostka Church.

Most of the headstones date back to the 1800s.

2

THE HOSPITAL AND ASYLUM

It was -17 degrees with the windchill as my friend and I crept through the halls of the dilapidated Fort Howard Veterans Hospital. I can never recall a time in my life where I had felt colder. My fingers were numb and my body felt as though it was on the brink of catching frostbite. This eerie feeling of coldness mirrored the emotional reaction we felt as we walked through this abandoned hospital. The once-sterile environment was covered in black mold, rust, decay, and fire damage after almost fifteen years of neglect. Fort Howard Veterans Hospital was once a place that saved lives and treated our nation's war heroes; now, it is simply forgotten about.

Fort Howard Veterans Hospital was constructed in 1940 on land that was previously used as a military base. In 1943, the hospital officially opened for patient care. After nearly sixty years in operation, it was determined that significant structural work was needed to update the main building. In June 2000, a plan was approved to redevelop Fort Howard into a continuing care retirement community for veterans through "Enhanced Use" legislation, upgrading the facility and expanding its use. Unfortunately, this plan never came to fruition, and in 2002, the facility was closed and the patients were transferred to other hospitals. Seventeen years later, the building sits in a state of deterioration and decay. Today, visitors to the area who attempt to see the building are greeted with tall fences, barb wire, surveillance cameras, and security guards.

The exterior of Fort Howard Veteran's Hospital.

An abandoned lighthouse sits out along the bay in front of the hospital.

Mold and moss overtake a waiting room.

Chipped paint cover one of the stairways.

Curtains still hang, blowing in the wind.

A door that had been completely smashed at one point.

The top section of an RV sits in front of the building.

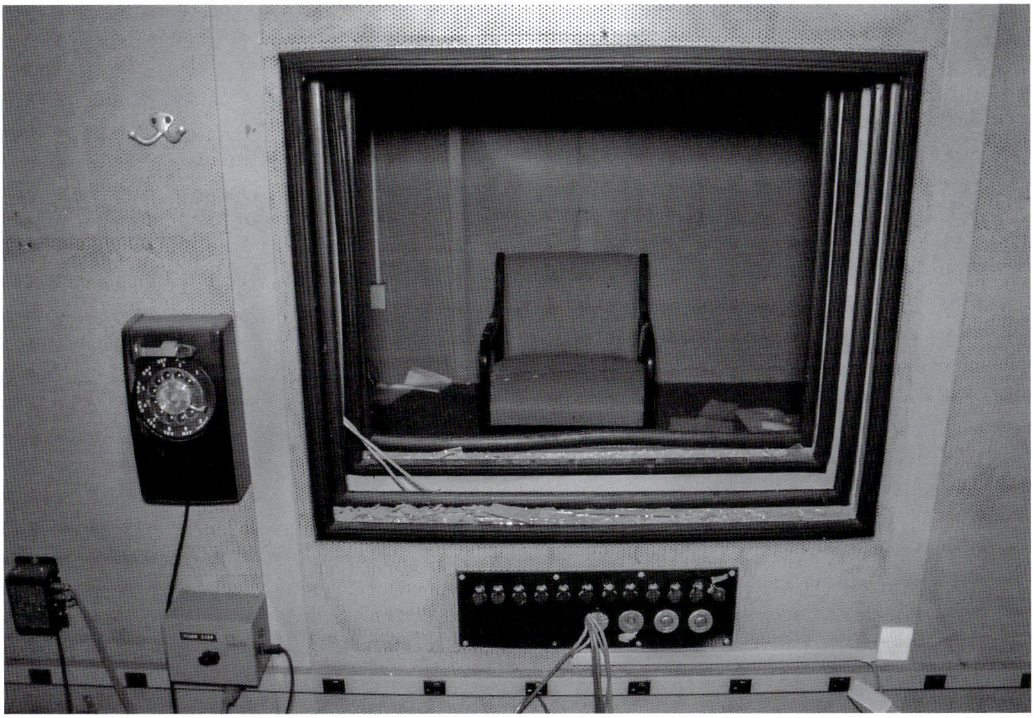

Here, family or doctors could communicate to an estranged patient while they are in confinement.

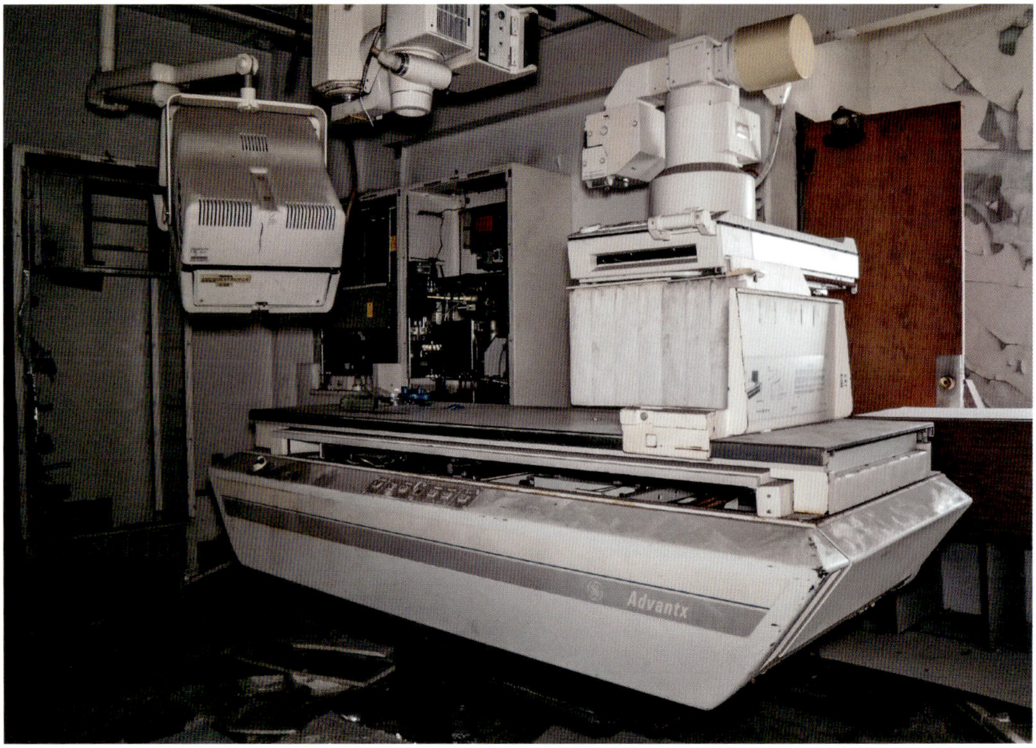

A full X-ray machine was left behind.

Stacks of old TVs sit in one of the lounges.

A fire destroyed a large part of the first floor.

Leave for your own safety—or what?

Time has been frozen inside the abandoned hospital.

Right: Medical machinery dangles from the ceiling.

Below: The morgue where dead bodies would have been stored.

Forest Haven Mental Asylum was the first abandoned place that I ever explored. At the age of sixteen, it was the most incredible and fascinating place I had ever been. Over time, it became a place for me to go back to and reminisce. With well over twenty trips to the asylum, I do not think there was ever a time when I did not discover something new about the place. Forest Haven will forever be a home to so many unforgettable memories. However, with its dark history, it makes you wonder why this place has not been demolished yet.

Built on the outskirts of Baltimore, Forest Haven was established in 1925 by the District of Columbia. The opening ceremony included a speech from First Lady Eleanor Roosevelt, who advocated for more hospitals to be built around the area. At the time, the facility was known as the "District Training School for the Mentally Retarded". The twenty-two-building facility was constructed across a 200-acre forest region, secluded from society. Forest Haven was praised at the time of its opening. Described as a "state-of-the-art" facility, much attention was focused on the asylum from the medical community at large. The facility quickly filled up with patients and overcrowding became an issue. This created numerous problems, to include funding issues, that would ultimately lead to its demise.

Forest Haven, overcrowded and underfunded, was unable to keep up with the introduction of new treatments and modern medicine. By the 1960s, the once-praised facility became more of a burden for the district. During one of the many financial shortfalls, a decision was made to terminate all educational and recreational programs at Forest Haven. Quality of life at the facility quickly began to degrade. In addition, the facility became the dumping ground of anyone deemed to have a learning disability. These individuals were identified and sent to this facility without going through proper evaluations, causing mentally healthy people to be entrapped at the asylum. The doctors at the facility would further exacerbate the situation through a regiment of treatments such as electroshock therapy.

In some cases, people who were deaf, illiterate, or even dyslectic were sent to Forest Haven to be institutionalized for treatment, as were those who spoke other languages. In a sick twist, people who were wrongfully sent there began to form conditions of mental instability due to the environment they were subjected to. The Curley Building, added to Forest Haven in 1971, provided care for male patients between the ages of ten to twenty-four; these patients were determined to need special attention.

Staffing was another issue the plagued the asylum. By 1972, there were over 100 positions not filled. In the same year, a case opened against Forest Haven revealing evidence of chronic mental, physical, and sexual abuse. The case began to gain further attention in 1977 after the mistreatment and deaths of patients began to surface. On June 14, 1978, Forest Haven was ordered to close and a declaration was made to prevent investment in improvements of the facility. However, this would only be the beginning of a long, drawn-out process, resulting in the relocation of around 1,300 patients.

By 1989, the population was reduced to around 252 patients. Living conditions were inhumane, and adequate health care was not being provided. Ten deaths occurred during this year, making it the deadliest year of the asylum's existence. After the first five deaths occurred, a judge ordered to force-close the facility. Deterioration of the facility had become unmanageable, and further budget cuts were made. Forest Haven finally closed in October 1991, and the remaining 233 patients were transferred to other locations.

Since the closing, different organizations attempted to make use of the buildings, but they all failed over time. The Forest Haven facilities were officially abandoned in 1998. A report in 2004 claimed that many of the buildings remained with running water and power. Records and private documents were all left behind in the buildings, exposing information that, by law, the facility was supposed to protect. A memorial known as "The Garden of Eternal Rest" can be found at the asylum, which acknowledges the lives of the known 387 patient lives that were lost there. Security regularly patrols Forest Haven Mental Asylum, and there are no known concrete plans for the property's future.

The main administration building of Forest Haven Mental Asylum.

A wheelchair sits out front.

The roof is slowly beginning to collapse due to age and neglect.

An old X-ray room.

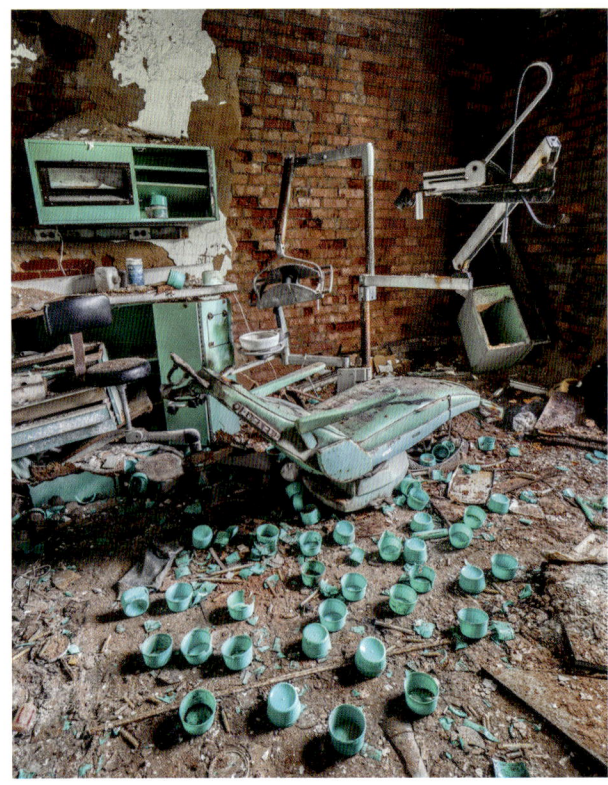

Cups scattered across the floor in front of a dentist chair inside one of the offices.

A rusty stretcher sitting in front of the asylum's morgue in the basement of the administration building.

A lonely desk sitting down a decayed hallway.

Suitcases stacked high, filled with clothes and belongings from patients.

Left: An old piano rotting away.

Below: Nature begins to overtake the old computers that have not been used in decades.

A Nike shoe sits in front of one of the many outdoor basketball courts at Forest Haven.

Forest Haven had its own powerplant so it could be completely independent from the outside world.

Another dentist chair still waiting to receive its next patient.

Many pillows lay on the ground of the gym that was inside the maximum-security building.

Right: An old tricycle that is missing its two back wheels.

Below: A dress still hangs waiting to be pressed.

Above: Industrial laundry machines with a labeled cart sitting in front.

Left: A vintage Pepsi machine sitting in the lounge of the administration building.

A record player that has long since played its last tune.

Another old Nike shoe sitting alone in one of the cottages.

3

REMAINS OF WAR

Many significant battles contributing to American history took place in and around the city of Baltimore. One of the most notable battles is Fort McHenry, which inspired the writing of the "Star-Spangled Banner" by Francis Scott Key. With military defense technology being very limited in comparison to what it is today, large concrete forts fitted with cannons were our best option for protecting the waters surrounding Baltimore.

Fort Armistead began to be built in 1897 and opened operations four years later in 1901. It was built as part of the Endicott Program, a $127-million defense spending plan passed by President Grover Cleveland to increase defense along the coast of America. After factoring inflation over time, that would be equivalent to a little over $3.2 billion. The fort was named in honor of George Armistead, who was commander of Fort McHenry during the War of 1812 when the British attacked. In 1917, after America entered World War I, many weapons were removed from the fort and transferred to a variety of other places out west, where it was determined that they could serve a better purpose.

In 1920, after the war, Fort Armistead closed. It would not be used again until 1952, when the Navy used it for ammunition storage through to 1954. Today, the fort has been converted into a public park. Upkeep of the fort itself has been lacking, resulting in trash accumulating and graffiti being painted all over the property. Local lore says that the fort has become a common meeting point for people to have romantic hookups. During my trip there, a parking lot with around six cars quickly cleared out when many noticed my camera. They all moved to various sides of the road further up from the fort where they could not be directly seen. When I walked through the facility's tunnels, I found used protection laying around along with different articles of clothing thrown about.

If you look out onto the Patapsco River from Fort Armistead, you can see the abandoned Fort Carroll. This fort was named after Charles Carroll, who was the last signer of the Declaration of Independence. Construction of the 3.4-acre artificial island began in 1848 by the United States Army Corps of Engineers. Designed by Colonel Robert E. Lee, it would have been the second defensive structure to sit between Baltimore and the Chesapeake Bay. Unfortunately, even though the fort had profound intentions, it was never completed or used as a fort. The most use made from it would be for storage of mines, holding sailors, and as a pistol range during the Spanish-American War. Facing the same fate as Fort Armistead, it was abandoned in 1920 and the steel used to construct portions of the fort was hauled away and used during the world wars.

After World War I, the United States had a surplus of Navy ships built in Baltimore. Many were discarded in Mallow's Bay. Curtis Creek is still home to a fascinating number of ship remains from across the time of America's history, spanning from before and after the world wars. A large ship that can still partially be seen is the *William T. Parker*. After being abandoned in around 1899, the ship sailed unmanned from the Outer Banks of North Carolina to the edge of Baltimore's harbor, where it was carried to shore by a tugboat and left to rot. In addition to the *William T. Parker*, a few other odds and ends of ships can be seen sticking out of the water. Curtis Creek is home to a lot of Baltimore history that has been forgotten about.

Across the river from Fort Armistead sits Fort Howard, originally known as North Point, which has a history many are unaware of. During the War of 1812, fifty British war ships arrived off the shores of Fort Howard. On September 12, 1814, the British attempted to invade North Point. The waters were too shallow for the ships to approach, causing their heavy artillery guns mounted to the ships to be ineffective. When the British troops advanced, they were met by American forces, who were able to defend the land, sending the troops retreating back to their ships.

Part of this same British fleet would fight two days later during the Battle of Fort McHenry and lose. Today, the fort remains as a concrete shell after being revamped in the late 1880s as part of the Endicott Program. The land would have many other uses before being converted into a public park. Adjacent to the fort sits the abandoned Fort Howard Veterans Hospital, mentioned earlier in this book.

Battery Winchester can be barely made out engraved above the Fort Armistead bunker.

Large canons used to sit ready to go at a moment's notice.

Time has taken a toll on the old fort.

The entrance inside the concrete structure.

Above: Graffiti covers the walls of the dark hallways.

Left: Hell is this way, if you are brave enough.

The abandoned Fort Carroll can be seen sitting out in the water from the shore of Fort Armistead.

The wooden ships have all mostly sunk over the years, but part of one remains standing.

A lower half of another ship can also still be seen.

These old ships have definitely seen their better days.

The back side of Fort Howard.

Even larger canons were once in place here.

Inside one of the bunkers.

4

SCHOOLS

After school buildings become abandoned, sometimes, they are lucky enough to earn a second life. They get converted into apartments, turned into other public spaces, or even converted into revitalized centers of education. Within the city of Baltimore, there are many abandoned schools that sit locked up with no plans for a future.

One school in particular that I had the chance to explore was abandoned, revitalized a number of years later into apartments, and then abandoned again. Originally, the building operated as an elementary school. After being closed, it was converted into supportive housing apartments in 2005. Much of what made it a school remained inside; lockers line the hallways, a gym and auditorium can be found on the first floor, empty trophy cases are located throughout, and more. I was unable to find much history about the complex. Today, you will find the facility boarded up, sitting in a state of abandonment. Metal scrappers have made their way into the building, along with many other vandals. During my visit, I was greeted by many vagrants who had made it their temporary home.

While public schools are often in transition, finding academies that have gone abandoned is typically not as common. This abandoned Catholic school was once an education center for hundreds of students before a lack of funds caused it to shut down permanently several years ago. Not much is left there to see; however, the school's worship room was quite interesting. Lined with stone, strips of blue stained glass illuminated the small room. With so many students, I was surprised it was not larger. The unique architecture of this space made it unlike any other abandoned religious room I had seen before.

Many of the windows have been boarded up at this abandoned school.

The first floor is themed blue with matching walls and lockers.

Right: The gymnasium, which has been covered in a graffiti piece.

Below: Toy cars and things sit scattered across the gym.

Above: The second floor has a green theme and held the daycare center.

Left: A tan, empty stairwell.

After being a school, this building served many other purposes before closing its doors.

A large painting full of color is still hung up inside the daycare room.

The auditorium of the school has remained untouched.

Right: The pews inside the worship room at the abandoned Christian school.

Below: Blue stained-glass windows illuminate the interior of the room.

5

ROWHOMES AND HOUSING

Baltimore is known for its abandoned rowhomes. They are literally everywhere. It is an epidemic that has caused the city many troubles throughout the past couple decades. A major decrease in population among other things are to blame for this issue. In 2010, city officials determined that there are 16,800 abandoned buildings in Baltimore. After tens of millions of dollars were invested to solve this issue, an updated city report in 2018 stated that there were still 16,500 vacant properties across the city.

As these places are torn down, more seem to go vacant all over the city. The city only counts properties that have had vacancy notices placed on them. The true number of vacant homes is estimated to be as high as 30,000 or more. During my journey through the lower parts of the city, I could not help but to notice an increase in abandoned homes than compared to the upper areas. Many streets of abandoned rowhomes were often accompanied by an also vacant factory or warehouse right around the corner. As places that once employed hundreds of surrounding workers go out of business, people are forced to find new places to live.

In addition to rowhomes, I discovered a few other homes throughout the city and outskirts. The first was a larger dilapidated home that had an old beach ball sitting in the snowy front yard. Inside, I came across a suitcase filled with old family photos, memories, and other things. In the woods behind an abandoned manufacturing facility, another abandoned house stood covered in ivy. The roof has since collapsed, but the stone and brick work remain and the home appears to be very old.

Known by local urban explorers as the Pink Room Mansion, this secluded house right outside the city was once home to a very wealthy doctor. Its Victorian-style architecture made it a very interesting house to explore. The home was complete with an indoor swimming pool and most of the furniture still relatively undisturbed inside. Unfortunately, as time passed, many vandals have since destroyed this once beautiful home. Graffiti can be found throughout the building, and a lot of the furniture has been broken. Exploring this place is like traveling through a time warp. The home would have been incredible in its day; today, the place is in disrepair, but leaves the explorer to imagine and appreciate what once was.

Only two rowhomes are still in use across the whole block.

Some rowhouses are torn down after the structure becomes too unstable.

No matter how big or small.

Even rowhomes with a unique style of architecture were still subjected to abandonment.

White boards cover this section of abandoned rowhomes

A snow-cone business sits at the end of this empty street.

Above: Fresh boards can be placed, but nothing else can be done for these dilapidated buildings.

Right: A reflection through a broken piece of a mirror laying on the sidewalk.

A lonely abandoned house sits on the corner of a street.

Large murals were painted to help boost moral and lighten up the city.

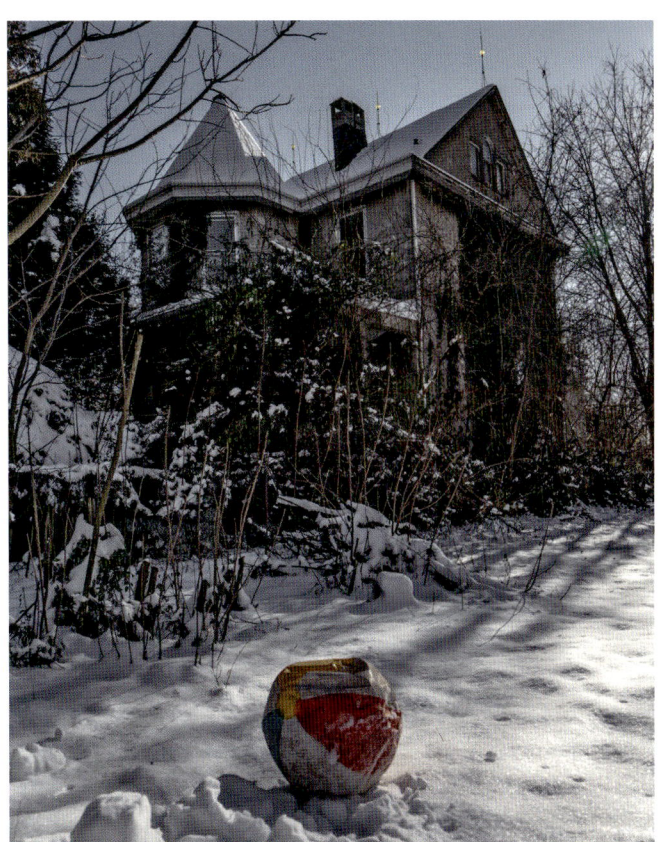

Right: A beach ball sits in front of this abandoned home.

Below: Family photos and memories are stored inside a suitcase in the house.

Left: The roof has caved in at this abandoned house.

Below: Nature has also begun to take over.

Elegant curtains covered in dust still hang in the window sill of this abandoned mansion.

A suitcase, carpet, and high school class photo are all that remain in the living room.

Above left: A toaster oven and blender sit plugged in, ready to make breakfast.

Above right: Graffiti covers the indoor abandoned swimming pool.

Below: The master bedroom remains almost spotless.

Above: What would have been a little girl's room.

Right: A creepy handmade clown sits on the floor.

6

INDUSTRIAL

Baltimore is a city full of industrial complexes. While many are still in use today, there are a number that have been abandoned over the years. These empty shells of buildings are perfect for redevelopment opportunities as they typically provide a lot of space to work with.

On the outskirts of Baltimore lies an abandoned Aerolab. Built around 1977, the lab provided the development and construction of wind tunnels for several years before the facility eventually closed. Heading into the complex, it was evident that the Aerolab had been completely disregarded. Trash littered the floor, a busted pipe flooded water in the bathroom, and an old shipping crate had been transformed into a residence for two homeless men, complete with a grill and everything. Not much remained of the business inside, other than an office space filled with books and manuals. A rusty imprint of where the letters were once placed marked where the Aerolab name was once displayed, facing the busy road next to the facility.

Savage Mill was a cotton mill originally established in the 1820s by Amos Williams and his brothers. After receiving raw cotton from the Port of Baltimore, it arrived at the mill by horse or ox wagon ready for use. Things such as tents and material for sails, among other things, were produced there for the military. During World War II, it is recorded that Savage Mill produced over 400,000 lb of canvas a month. The mill ceased operations in the 1950s and was bought by a plastics company. Today, the main building has been converted into a unique shopping area where local artisans sell their work next to specialty shops and restaurants.

Although the larger building has been restored, the part of the mill that provided power to the facility sits abandoned. This section of the structure sits along the Little Patuxent River. Tall brick walls standing along with massive industrial metal parts remain in place. When you are standing inside this portion of the mill, you get a great view of the river. On one of the large turbines, "adventure awaits" had been written, which reminded me of why I explore. Helen Keller once said, "Life is either a daring adventure, or nothing," which is an idea that resonates loudly inside me.

At one point, grain accounted for one-fifth of Baltimore's exports. Today, only one grain elevator remains operational in the city. I had the chance to explore a grain elevator that closed in 1994. The one I explored has been used as a set for several movies and TV shows. Coming upon the large structure, you feel as if you have just arrived at an evil fortress. This is due to its size and dark, depressing complexion. The wide-open floors and intense piping made it to be unlike any other abandoned industrial building I had seen before. A local worker gave me a tour of the place, knowing the way around like the back of his hand. The building is fenced, secured, and not open to the public, but I was lucky enough to get a chance to look at the history that has been left behind.

Left: Self portrait of myself sitting on the stairs at the abandoned Aerolab.

Below: A lot of trash and things are all over the floor of the delivery bay.

A makeshift basketball hoop.

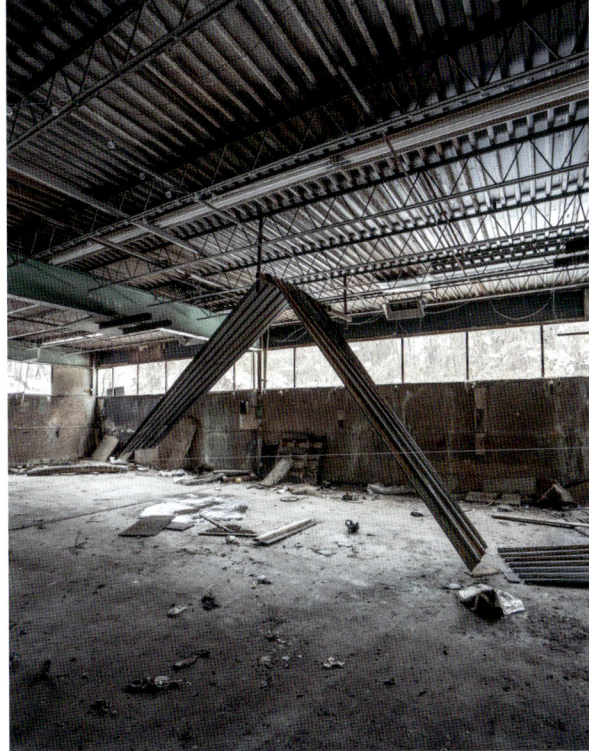

Large sheets of metal roofing have fallen overtime due to neglect.

An empty barrel sits on the ground.

This would have helped workers pick up and carry the heavy things to bring it from one side to the other.

Right: The controls to move the winch.

Below: A large wooden cabinet that has fallen over on the second floor.

Above: Looking out one of the broken windows.

Left: Manuals among other things cover the office floors.

The old, wooden spiral staircase.

The exterior of the Areolab from the back parking lot.

Much of Savage Mill has collapsed over the years, but this wall still stands strong.

A view of the mill from across the creek.

Some of the inner workings still remain.

Adventure awaits written on the snow-covered generator.

Water would have flowed through here at one point, but it has been sealed off since.

More rusty remains of the mill.

Vandals have covered many parts in graffiti.

A view of the creek from inside the mill.

Above: This would have generated the power for Savage Mill.

Left: Looking up at the cloudy sky.

The abandoned grain elevator in all its glory.

A view of the shipyard from the top of the building.

These pipes reminded me of a gas mask.

An empty barrel that probably was full of grain at one point.

The massive pipes that flowed throughout the building.

Sun shines through, allowing light to shine on this industrial wasteland.

Remove dust from clothing before entering.

Sixth floor, pipes number ninety-two through ninety-five.

The large pipe breaks off into three sections.

7

BUSINESS AND MORE

Throughout the city of Baltimore, there are many businesses and other places that have closed over the years and currently sit in a state of decay. In most extreme cases, the buildings begin to collapse on themselves as nature reclaims its land. Banks that once were renowned institutions with state-of-the-art safes sit empty and unused. Grocery stores that could provide a variety of goods to the people around them become cinder-blocked wastes of space. Many of these buildings have unique opportunities to be redeveloped, but instead, they are going to be demolished or continue to be neglected.

Built in 1906, the Bay Shore Amusement Park provided recreation and a relaxing environment right outside the city of Baltimore. Once accessible by trolley, the park featured many amenities, such as a dance hall, bowling alley, restaurant, and pier. Bethlehem Steel Company bought the land in the 1940s and demolished the park. In 1987, the Maryland Department of Natural Resources bought the land and converted it into a state park. Today, a concrete shell of the powerplant that powered the amusement park still remains along with the pier that has been broken up at its entrance to prevent people from going out on it. The park plans to demolish these remains, which will erase the last remains of Bay Shore Amusement Park.

The Baltimore Behavioral Health center, which provided care and treatment to many, filed for bankruptcy in 2012 after owing millions. The former CEO was charged with fraud, and the facility was closed. Fresh boarded up doors and windows compliment the complex architecture of the building. Located just around the corner from University of Maryland, the old Baltimore Behavioral Health center offers a prime location that surprisingly no one has acted upon. The inside was already falling apart during my visit, looking as if it had sat empty for decades.

Throughout the city, historical brick fire houses, built as early as the mid-1800s, can be found. While many are still in use or repurposed, there are still a number of fire houses that sit abandoned. These buildings played a vital role to the protection of the city so the incidences such as the Great Baltimore Fire of 1904 did not repeat itself. Standing out with their unique design, these buildings are historical landmarks that should not be forgotten. The city has sent out many proposals to the public for these buildings to be bought and put back into use again.

Above: The exterior of the abandoned North Point powerplant.

Left: Painters have turned this concrete shell into their canvas.

A recreation of van Gogh's *The Starry Night*.

All the machinery inside has been removed.

A spooky skull pumpkin painted on the wall.

The abandoned pier that sits a little way down from the powerplant.

An abandoned Super Pride grocery store.

An abandoned behavioral health center.

91

The vault inside an abandoned bank.

Above: Castle-like architecture of an abandoned firehouse.

Right: Another one of the many abandoned firehouses within Baltimore.

A tree growing out of the side of an abandoned warehouse.

Opposite page: An abandoned police station sits boarded up on the corner of a street.

BIBLIOGRAPHY

Duncan, I., 'In 2010, Baltimore had 16,800 vacants. Eight years and millions of dollars later, the number is down to 16,500', *The Baltimore Sun,* April 26, 2018

Grant, R., 'Daniels', *Atlas Obscura,* from atlasobscura.com/places/daniels

Kilar, S., 'Baltimore Behavioral Health files for bankruptcy', *The Baltimore Sun,* December 31, 2012

Kinling, N., 'St. Mary's College', *Atlas Obscura,* from atlasobscura.com/places/st-mary-s-college

Linnea, H., 'Curtis Creek Ship Graveyard', *Atlas Obscura,* from atlasobscura.com/places/curtis-creek-ship-graveyard

North Point State Park, 'Park History', from northpointstatepark.homestead.com/history.html

Preservation Alliance of Baltimore County, 'Fort Carroll', from explore.baltimore-heritage.org/items/show/231

Sherman, N., 'City goes real estate agent, pitching 'eclectic' surplus property', *The Baltimore Sun,* June 10, 2014

Sometimes Interesting, 'Abandoned Home for the Abandoned: Forest Haven Asylum', from sometimes-interesting.com/2014/04/12/abandoned-home-for-the-abandoned-forest-haven-asylum/

Soo Hoo, W., 'At Maryland's Savage Mill, history and commerce converge', *The Washington Post,* April 28, 2016

U.S Department of Veteran Affairs, 'History of the Fort Howard VA Campus', from maryland.va.gov/about/History_of_the_Fort_Howard.asp

Wooton, S., 'GRAIN ELEVATOR SHUTS DOWN', *The Baltimore Sun,* August 31, 1994